POKÉMON ADVENTURES:
DIAMOND AND PEARL/
PLATINUM
Volume 10
VIZ Media Edition

Story by **HIDENORI KUSAKA**
Art by **SATOSHI YAMAMOTO**

© 2014 The Pokémon Company International.
© 1995–2011 Nintendo / Creatures Inc. / GAME FREAK inc.
TM, ®, and character names are trademarks of Nintendo.
POCKET MONSTERS SPECIAL Vol. 10 (39)
by Hidenori KUSAKA, Satoshi YAMAMOTO
© 1997 Hidenori KUSAKA, Satoshi YAMAMOTO
All rights reserved.
Original Japanese edition published by SHOGAKUKAN.
English translation rights in the United States of America, Canada, the United Kingdom,
Ireland, Australia, New Zealand and India arranged with SHOGAKUKAN.

Translation/Tetsuichiro Miyaki
English Adaptation/Bryant Turnage
Touch-up & Lettering/Annaliese Christman
Design/Yukiko Whitley
Editor/Annette Roman

Printed in the U.S.A.

Published by VIZ Media, LLC
P.O. Box 77010
San Francisco, CA 94107

10 9 8 7 6 5 4
First printing, February 2014
Fourth printing, June 2019

VIZ MEDIA
viz.com

Our Story So Far…

A story about young people entrusted with Pokédexes by the world's leading Pokémon Researchers. Together with their Pokémon, they travel, battle, and evolve!

Dia

HE LOVES FOOD AND IS THE FUNNY MAN IN HIS COMEDY DUO WITH HIS FRIEND PEARL. DIA IS KIND AND QUIET, BUT ALSO HAS GREAT INNER STRENGTH.

Pearl

THE STRAIGHT MAN IN HIS COMEDIC DUO WITH HIS FRIEND DIA. IMPATIENT AND STRONG-WILLED. BY NATURE WATCHFUL, HE HAS TAKEN ON A COMMANDING ROLE DURING THEIR JOURNEY WITH LADY.

Lady

PLATINUM "LADY" BERLITZ IS A STUDIOUS GIRL FROM A WEALTHY, ARISTOCRATIC FAMILY WHO IS RAPIDLY IMPROVING AS A POKÉMON TRAINER BECAUSE LADY IS FINALLY ABLE TO PRACTICE THE TECHNIQUES SHE HAS READ ABOUT IN BOOKS. SHE IS CURRENTLY CHALLENGING TRAINERS AT THE BATTLE FRONTIER.

Dahlia

THE PROTECTOR OF THE BATTLE ROULETTE, AKA, THE ARCADE STAR.

Darach

CAITLIN'S VALET, THE CASTLE BUTLER.

Caitlin

THE OWNER OF THE BATTLE CASTLE. SHE LOOKS DELICATE, BUT IS SHE...?

Looker

AN INTERNATIONAL POLICE OFFICER. HE IS STRIVING HARD TO INFILTRATE TEAM GALACTIC.

Riley
THE MAN FROM IRON ISLAND WHO TRAINED DIA. AN AURA WIELDER.

Palmer
THE TOWER TYCOON AND THE ONE WHO PRESIDES OVER THE FIVE FRONTIER BRAINS AND FACILITIES.

Argenta
THE HALL MATRON AND A SKILLED TRAINER WHO PROTECTS THE BATTLE HALL.

Thorton
THE FRONTIER BRAIN OF THE BATTLE FACTORY AND THE FACTORY HEAD.

THE BATTLE AT THE SPEAR PILLAR HAS ENDED, AND LADY AND HER FRIENDS ARE TRIUMPHANT. HOWEVER, JUST WHEN DIA AND PEARL THINK THEY CAN RELAX, A PORTAL TO A MYSTERIOUS DOMAIN OPENS UP IN FRONT OF THEM AND DIALGA, PALKIA AND EVEN CYRUS ARE DRAGGED INTO THE VOID!

EAGER TO DISCOVER THE WHEREABOUTS OF LADY'S MISSING BODYGUARDS PAKA AND UJI, OUR FRIENDS TRY TO DECODE THE MEANING OF CHARON'S CRYPTIC COMMENT ABOUT THE "OTHER SIDE OF THE WORLD." TO GATHER MORE INFORMATION, DIA AND PEARL HEAD OUT ON THEIR OWN AGAIN IN SEARCH OF THE OTHER LEGENDARY POKÉMON, WHILE LADY HEADS DOWN TO THE BATTLE ZONE LOCATED OUTSIDE OF SINNOH.

JOINED BY INTERNATIONAL POLICE AGENT LOOKER, LADY TAKES ON THE CHALLENGE OF THE FIVE BATTLE FRONTIER FACILITIES IN HOPES OF EARNING THE PRIVILEGE TO ASK THE FRONTIER BRAINS WHO RUN THEM QUESTIONS ABOUT THE PLACE PAKA AND UJI HAVE BEEN TRANSPORTED TO. AS LADY RACKS UP VICTORIES, A BOY NAME BUCK MEETS WITH HER AND LOOKER. WHEN THEY TELL BUCK THAT TEAM GALACTIC IS UP TO SOMETHING AT STARK MOUNTAIN, HE HEADS OUT THERE ALONE TO INVESTIGATE, DESPITE THE DANGER...

Cyrus
TEAM GALACTIC'S BOSS, WHO WAS DRAGGED INTO A MYSTERIOUS REALM. WHAT HAPPENED TO HIM NEXT...?

Charon
A TEAM GALACTIC COMMANDER AND SCIENTIST WHO IS PASSIONATE ABOUT HIS LEGENDARY POKÉMON RESEARCH.

Volkner
ONE OF THE SINNOH GYM LEADERS WHO VISITED FLINT. WHAT WAS HE AFTER...?

Flint
ONE OF THE SINNOH ELITE FOUR. A CAREFREE FIRE TYPE POKÉMON EXPERT.

LADY'S POKÉMON

LOPUNNY (LOPUNNY, ♀)
MILD. ALERT TO SOUNDS.

EMPOLEON (EMPOLEON, ♀)
SERIOUS. A LITTLE QUICK TEMPERED.

RAPIDASH (RAPIDASH, ♂)
MODEST. OFTEN LOST IN THOUGHT.

PLATINUM

DIA'S POKÉMON

(MAMOSWINE, ♂)

DON (BASTIODON, ♂)
CAREFUL. SOMEWHAT STUBBORN.

TRU (TORTERRA, ♂)
RELAXED. GOOD PERSEVERANCE.

REGIGIGAS

KIT (LICKILICKY, ♂)
BOLD. SCATTERS THINGS OFTEN.

LAX (MUNCHLAX, ♂)
IMPISH. LOVES TO EAT.

DIAMOND

PEARL'S POKÉMON

ER (TAUROS, ♂)

RAYLER (LUXRAY, ♂)
BRAVE. THOROUGHLY CUNNING.

CHIMLER (INFERNAPE, ♂)
NAUGHTY. LIKES TO RUN.

ER (DIGLETT, ♂)

ZELLER (BUIZEL, ♂)
STUBBORN. LIKES TO FIGHT.

CHATLER (CHATOT, ♂)
HASTY. SOMEWHAT OF A CLOWN.

PEARL

POKÉMON

ADVENTURES
Diamond and Pearl
PLATINUM

10

CONTENTS

PLATINUM

POKÉMON

Adventure 86 • Tackling Togekiss

THERE ARE EVEN SOME THAT AN OLD WOMAN LIKE ME HAS NEVER HEARD OF BEFORE.

THERE ARE THOSE WHOSE NAMES HAVE PASSED DOWN TO US THROUGH THE GENERATIONS AND THOSE WHO ONLY EXIST IN LEGENDS.

WHAT A SURPRISE!

I HAD NO IDEA THERE WERE SO MANY OF THEM...

WHAT DO THEY INTEND TO DO WITH ALL OF THESE POKÉMON NOW?

THEY HAVE JUST SUMMONED DIALGA AND PALKIA... THEY COULD HAVE VAPORIZED ALL OF SINNOH...

AND THIS MAN NAMED CHARON...

TEAM GALACTIC...

ISN'T IT OBVIOUS?

FWP

WHY ARE THEY OBSESSED WITH CONTROLLING THE WORLD?

THEY WANT TO HAVE THOSE POKÉMON ALL TO THEMSELVES.

10

ALL THREE OF THE POKÉMON ARE ON THE MEND AND DOING WELL.

DAY 18...

DON'T WORRY. IT'LL TAKE A LITTLE MORE TIME, BUT THEY'LL RECOVER. I PROMISE.

HOW ARE THEY DOING?

EXCUSE ME... I'M PEARL.

AND I'M DIA-MOND.

THE GYM LEADERS ENTRUSTED THESE POKÉMON TO THEIR CURRENT TRAINER, CORRECT? BUT IS SHE ABLE TO MAKE GOOD USE OF THEM?

I'M SO GLAD...

IF YOUR LITTLE BROTHER WERE HERE, HE'D SO WANT TO HAVE A POKÉMON BATTLE WITH HER, DAISY.

OH MY!

ABSOLUTELY! LADY BEAT ALL THE GYM LEADERS! THAT'S HOW THEY KNEW SHE COULD HANDLE THEM!

THERE ARE PEOPLE WE STILL NEED TO SAVE!

AND WE CAN'T SAY THAT WE'VE EXACTLY **SOLVED** THE PROBLEM YET.

OH, NOT **ME**.

YOU DID?

...WE BORROWED THEM FROM PROFESSOR ROWAN AND EXAMINED THEM CAREFULLY.

...CHARON'S NOTES...

THAT NOTEBOOK YOU GOT AHOLD OF DURING THE BATTLE AT THE SPEAR PILLAR...

AND I'LL HELP YOU ANY WAY I CAN.

YES, I'VE HEARD ALL ABOUT IT.

AND AARON.

LUCIAN.

BERTHA.

THE GREATEST TRAINERS IN THE SINNOH REGION...

...THE ELITE FOUR.

GOOD. VERY GOOD!!

HUH?

BATTLE 20, WON!!

I HOPE HE'S ALL RIGHT!

I CAN'T HELP THINKING ABOUT THAT KID BACK ON THE MOUNTAIN...

HMM...

BUT...

THAT'S GREAT...

THE NEXT BATTLE IS AGAINST THE FRONTIER BRAIN.

YO

YO

YO

YO

...BETTER STOP THE WHEEL... THERE!

SO...

...WHATEVER THEY ARE, THEY'LL HAVE A PROBLEM USING THEM IF THEY'RE PARALYZED.

I DON'T KNOW WHAT MOVES THEY USE, BUT...

DAHLIA'S POKÉMON ARE LUDICOLO, MEDICHAM AND TOGEKISS...

BATTLE FRONTIER RULE BOOK

THERE ARE FIVE TYPES OF FACILITIES, EACH WITH A DIFFERENT TYPE OF POKÉMON BATTLE. THE BATTLES ARE FOUGHT ACCORDING TO STRICT RULES. HERE IS SOME MORE DETAILED INFORMATION ABOUT THE RULES AT VARIOUS FACILITIES.

DIRECTIONS

▲ LOCATED TOWARDS THE WEST OF THE BATTLE FRONTIER ENTRANCE.

FACILITY RULES
BATTLE CASTLE ①

IN THE BATTLE CASTLE, YOU BORROW EQUIPMENT AND ITEMS, AS WELL AS GATHER INFORMATION ON YOUR OPPONENTS BEFORE YOUR FIGHT. IN ORDER TO DO THAT, YOU NEED TO HAVE EARNED CP (CASTLE POINTS). IN THIS FACILITY, YOU NEED THE SKILL TO MANAGE (SAVE AND SPEND) YOUR CP WISELY.

TYPE OF BATTLE	NUMBER OF PARTICIPATING POKÉMON	TO RECEIVE THE COMMEMORATIVE PRINT, YOU WILL NEED...
SINGLE	3 POKÉMON (ALL DIFFERENT TYPES)	7 × 3 SETS =
DOUBLE	4 POKÉMON (ALL DIFFERENT TYPES)	21 CONSECUTIVE WINS

■CP■

YOU START OUT WITH 10. YOU RECEIVE MORE CP EVERY TIME YOU WIN A BATTLE. YOU GET BONUS POINTS FOR WINNING IN A NICE WAY...FOR EXAMPLE, BY NOT KNOCKING OUT ALL OF THE OPPONENT'S POKÉMON OR BY NOT GETTING YOUR POKÉMON TOO INJURED.

OWNER **CAITLIN**
FRONTIER BRAIN **DARACH**

EMPOLEON, DRILL PECK!!

I CAN DRAW OUT THE FULL POTENTIAL OF OTHER PEOPLE'S POKÉMON DURING A FIGHT.

CRASH

BUT IT APPEARS THAT VICTORY IS SMILING UPON THE FRONTIER BRAIN AT THE BITTER END.

THE CHALLENGER MANAGED TO SPIN THE ROULETTE WHEEL TO HER ADVANTAGE UNTIL NOW.

BUT THE CHALLENGER CAN'T HELP BUT HESITATE BECAUSE SHE'S FACING HER OWN POKÉMON.

THE FRONTIER BRAIN HAS NO QUALMS ABOUT CONTINUING HER VIGOROUS ATTACK.

OH MY. THE CHALLENGER IS AT A REAL DISADVANTAGE NOW.

THA WAS SUPE EFFE TIVE

I HAVE TO...

WHAT TWO?

HELP WHO?

...TRAPPED IN THERE.

I KNOW THEY'RE...

THAT'S THE ONLY REASON I CAME TO THE BATTLE ZONE.

AND TO HELP THEM, I HAVE TO GET INFORMATION FROM THESE TRAINERS HERE.

I **HAVE** TO!

I WANT TO **GO** THERE MYSELF!

NO... I DON'T JUST WANT TO LEARN ABOUT IT...

I WANT TO LEARN WHAT I NEED TO KNOW ABOUT THE DISTORTION WORLD AS SOON AS I CAN!

I HAVE TO GO AND HELP THOSE TWO!!

EVEN IF... I MUST FIGHT MY **OWN** POKÉMON!

AND THAT'S WHY I CAN'T AFFORD TO LOSE.

...AND NEVER BACK DOWN!

DON'T EVER GIVE UP...

CAN YOU TAKE A LOOK AT THE AURA OF THE THREE POKÉMON IN FRONT OF YOU?

MEDICHAM, YOU'VE HONED YOUR MIND TO SEE THE AURA OF YOUR OPPONENTS...

NOD

DO THEY HAVE A FIGHTING AURA?

OKAY THEN!

I GUESS I DIDN'T EVEN HAVE TO ASK...

KRCK

BUCK

LOUD SPEAKER!

EQUIPMENT NO. 9

ACK!

HMM...

KLTTR KLTTR

BUCK!! BUCK?!

ARE YOU OKAY?

BUC

BUT IT LOOKS LIKE I'M GONNA NEED YOUR HELP AFTER ALL...

HEH... HEH... SORRY, MISTER.

I TOLD YOU I DIDN'T WANT YOU SNOOPING AROUND...

PANT

PANT

PANT

I THOUGHT...

WELL... THAT WAS MY INTENTION, ANYWAY.

...IF THE BAD GUYS WERE AFTER THE TREASURE, I'D PLACE IT UNDER MY PROTECTION.

AND INDEED, YOU WERE RIGHT!

THAT STONE MIGHT HAVE BEEN PLACED THERE TO **SEAL** SOMETHING OFF...

AND THAT'S WHEN I REALIZED...

RIGHT... IT SEEMED LIKE A MASSIVE AMOUNT OF ENERGY WAS UNLEASHED.

SO THA WAS T FIRS TREM I FEL

BATTLE FRONTIER RULE BOOK

THERE ARE FIVE TYPES OF FACILITIES, EACH WITH A DIFFERENT TYPE OF POKÉMON BATTLE. THE BATTLES ARE FOUGHT ACCORDING TO STRICT RULES. HERE IS SOME MORE DETAILED INFORMATION ABOUT THE RULES AT VARIOUS FACILITIES.

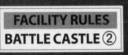

FACILITY RULES
BATTLE CASTLE ②

How to use your CP

■ USE YOUR CP TO LEARN ABOUT YOUR OPPONENT ■

GATHER INFORMATION ON YOUR OPPONENT'S POKÉMON BEFORE THE FIGHT.

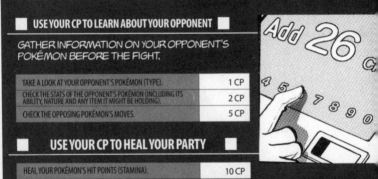

TAKE A LOOK AT YOUR OPPONENT'S POKÉMON (TYPE).	1 CP
CHECK THE STATS OF THE OPPONENT'S POKÉMON (INCLUDING ITS ABILITY, NATURE AND ANY ITEM IT MIGHT BE HOLDING).	2 CP
CHECK THE OPPOSING POKÉMON'S MOVES.	5 CP

■ USE YOUR CP TO HEAL YOUR PARTY ■

HEAL YOUR POKÉMON'S HIT POINTS (STAMINA).	10 CP

YOU CAN ONLY RESTORE YOUR POKÉMON'S HIT POINTS AT THE BEGINNING. BUT AS YOU CONTINUE WITH THE CHALLENGES AND RAISE YOUR RANK, YOU CAN USE YOUR CP TO RESTORE OTHER THINGS.

■ RANKING UP ■

RANKING UP CAN ALSO BE ACHIEVED BY GATHERING CP. APART FROM HEALING YOUR POKÉMON, RANKING UP ALSO AFFECTS THE ITEMS YOU CAN RENT. IN THE BEGINNING, YOU CAN ONLY RENT 8 KINDS OF BERRIES, BUT AFTER RANKING UP THAT GROWS TO 8 KINDS OF BERRIES + 12 KINDS OF ITEMS AND THEN 32 KINDS OF BERRIES + 27 KINDS OF ITEMS, ENABLING YOU TO BROADEN YOUR STRATEGY.

POKéMON
ADVENTURES

WZZW

FWOOT

KLTTR KLTTR

RMBL

NOW TELL ME WHY YOU TRIED TO CAPTURE HEATRAN.

OKAY, CHARON...

I DID IT! I FOUND IT MISTER!

WELL DONE!

RIP

ANSWER ME!

HEY...

...THOR-TON!

CAN YOU HEAR ME? IT'S ME, DAHLIA!

...I WAS JUST TALKING ABOUT THE DISTORTION WORLD WITH ANOTHER FRONTIER BRAIN THE OTHER DAY.

REALLY?

COME TO THINK OF IT...

WHO?

YOU SHOULD TALK TO HIM YOUR-SELF—IN PERSON!

COME ON! FOLLOW ME...

STAFF ONLY OFF LIMITS

BLIP BLIP

WOW.

AND THE MAN IS PALMER FROM THE BATTLE TOWER.

THE WOMAN IS ARGENTA FROM THE BATTLE HALL.

UMM... WERE THE OTHER PEOPLE WITH HIM FRONTIER BRAINS TOO?

THAT'S RIGHT.

'T'S INE.

I'M SORRY YOU DIDN'T GET A CHANCE TO TALK TO THORTON PROPERLY.

Hm.

THAT'S ODD... THEY SHOULD ALL BE AT THEIR FACILITIES AT THIS TIME OF DAY...

AH, THAT'S THE SPIRIT! GOOD LUCK!

I'LL GET A CHANCE TO TALK TO HIM THEN—IF I BEAT HIM!

I WAS GOING TO BATTLE AT THE BATTLE FACTORY SOON ANYWAY...

THANK YOU FOR ALL YOUR HELP, DAHLIA!

THE REASON I CHOSE THE BATTLE FACTORY NEXT IS BECAUSE...

...IT'S A FACILITY WHERE YOU FIGHT WITH RENTAL POKÉMON.

SO I DON'T HAVE TO USE MY OWN POKÉMON THERE.

LET'S HEAD OVER TO THE BATTLE FACTORY!

NOW THE...

YOU'RE ONLY GOING THERE BECAUSE YOU THINK THORTON HAS SOME USEFUL INFORMATION FOR YOU?

NO.

WHY THEN?

POKÉMON STORAGE SYSTEM CORNER

...THAT THEIR TREATMENT IS FINISHED.

AND I WAS JUST NOTIFIED...

POP POP POP

BOM

BOM

BOM

THE TIME HAS COME!

CHERRIM, FROSLASS PACHIRISU!

FOOOSH

TIP

FOOSH

LET'S SEE... THAT FORRE- TRESS!

AND OUT OF THOSE THREE, I'LL TAKE...

LET'S TRADE! I'M GOING TO LET MY WORM- ADAM GO.

HURRAY, I WON!

Welcome to the Battle Factory.

SKREEEE

At the Battle Factory, you compete against your opponents using rented Pokémon.

In this facility, you may not use your own Pokémon. Is that acceptable to you?

...OF NOT BEING ALLOWED TO USE MY OWN POKÉMON AT THE BATTLE ARCADE.

OF COURSE! I'VE ALREADY EXPERIENCED THE DIFFICULTY...

'SKREECH'

Then please move ahead to the arena.

FOOOM

Please choose three Pokémon.

RTTL RTTL FLK

SINGLE.

Which challenge would you like to accept?
Single Battle
Double Battle
Read Instructions

PING

Level 50
Open Level
Quit

LEVEL 50 PLEASE.

HEY, PALMER! THIS IS NO TIME TO CHILL AND OBSERVE A BATTLE! WE NEED TO FIGURE OUT WHY THE COMMUNICA-TION DEVICES ARE MALFUNC-TIONING!

THE CHALLENGER WHO DEFEATED DARACH AND DAHLIA...

...AND IS ALREADY ON HER WAY TO FACE THORTON, THE THIRD FRONTIER BRAIN.

SO, THAT'S HER...

GHT. RRY.

BATTLE FRONTIER RULE BOOK

THERE ARE FIVE TYPES OF FACILITIES, EACH WITH A DIFFERENT TYPE OF POKÉMON BATTLE. THE BATTLES ARE FOUGHT ACCORDING TO STRICT RULES. HERE IS SOME MORE DETAILED INFORMATION ABOUT THE RULES AT VARIOUS FACILITIES.

FACILITY RULES
BATTLE ARCADE

THE BATTLE ARCADE IS A FACILITY WHERE YOU SPIN A HUGE ROULETTE WHEEL TO CHOOSE WHAT KIND OF SITUATION YOU WILL BATTLE IN. THE IMAGES ON THE PANELS OF THE WHEEL DETERMINE THE SITUATION.

TYPE OF BATTLE	NUMBER OF PARTICIPATING POKÉMON	TO RECEIVE THE COMMEMORATIVE PRINT, YOU WILL NEED...
SINGLE	3 POKÉMON (ALL DIFFERENT TYPES)	7 × 3 SETS =
DOUBLE	4 POKÉMON (ALL DIFFERENT TYPES)	21 CONSECUTIVE WINS

■ THE TYPES OF PANELS AND WHAT THEY SYMBOLIZE ■

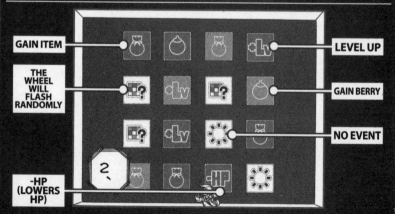

GAIN ITEM

THE WHEEL WILL FLASH RANDOMLY

-HP (LOWERS HP)

LEVEL UP

GAIN BERRY

NO EVENT

◄ LOCATED TO THE EAST OF THE BATTLE FRONTIER ENTRANCE— THE BUILDING WITH THE BEAUTIFUL DÉCOR.

APART FROM THE PANELS INTRODUCED ON THE RIGHT, THERE ARE ALSO WEATHER AND STATUS CONDITION PANELS. WHEN THE ROULETTE STOPS ON ONE OF THOSE PANELS, YOU MUST FIGHT UNDER THOSE CIRCUMSTANCES.

▲ ALL OF YOUR POKÉMON ARE POISONED.

▼ A PANEL THAT TURNS THE WEATHER TO RAIN.

◄ EXCHANGE POKÉMON WITH YOUR OPPONENT FOR THIS BATTLE.

■ RED FIELD AND BLACK FIELD ■

FOR THIS BATTLE, EACH PARTICIPANT STANDS UPON A FIELD COLORED IN RED OR BLACK. THE GAIN BERRY, GAIN ITEM, AND RECEIVE POISON PANELS ARE ALSO IN THOSE COLORS. THE RED PANELS AFFECT THE TRAINER ON THE RED FIELD AND THE BLACK PANELS AFFECT THE TRAINER ON THE BLACK FIELD.

■ DURATION OF EVENTS (EFFECTS) ■

THE EVENTS UPON THE PANELS WILL EITHER AFFECT THE TRAINER FOR ONE BATTLE OR FOR THE WHOLE SET, WHICH CONSISTS OF SEVEN BATTLES. THE ACQUISITION OF BERRIES AND ITEMS WILL ALSO AFFECT THE ENTIRE SET, WHILE EVERYTHING ELSE WILL ONLY AFFECT A SINGLE BATTLE.

FRONTIER BRAIN **ARCADE STAR: DAHLIA**

POKÉMON
Adventures

Adventure 90 ● Uprooting Seedot

...THE REALLY SCARY THING ABOUT THE MOVE TOXIC SPIKES IS THAT IT STINGS AND POISONS THE SWITCHED POKÉMON.

JUUUGGH

EEEE!

PATH WUMP

THE SIXTH BATTLE OF THE SECOND SET— VICTORY!!

HOORAY!!

PLATINUM BERLITZ!

BESIDES, I HAVE TIME, SINCE THE BATTLE ARCADE IS CLOSED.

I JUST HAD TO COME AND WATCH...

WHAT ARE **YOU** DOING HERE? YOU'RE SUPPOSED TO BE AT THE BATTLE ARCADE!

CLOSED?!

HEY!

THE WINNER IS ALLOWED TO REPLACE ONE OF THEIR THREE POKÉMON WITH ONE OF THEIR OPPONENT'S POKÉMON.

...VERY CARE-FULLY.

SHE'S CHOOS-ING...

TRADING IS A UNIQUE FEATURE OF THE...

...BATTLE FAC-TORY.

WELL THEN...

IN RETURN, I'LL TAKE KADABRA FROM MY OPPONENT'S RENTAL POKÉMON.

I'M GOING TO LET GO OF GRIMER.

...THIS FACILITY'S FRONTIER BRAIN!

JUST ONE MORE SET UNTIL I FACE...

AS A MATTER OF FACT, IT ISN'T EVEN IN THE FRONTIER AREA...

WE KNOW WE'RE BEING JAMMED—AND WE HAVE A GOOD IDEA FROM WHERE.

WE HAVE RILEY TO THANK FOR THIS. THORTON'S STRANGE MACHINE ISN'T THE REASON BEHIND THE MALFUNCTION-ING OF THIS COMMUNICA-TION DEVICE.

RIGHT.

I GUESS WE WERE WRONG TO SUSPECT THORTON.

WELL...

SOME-WHERE FAR OFF TO THE NORTH...

IT'S FROM SOME-WHERE FAR AWAY...

... LOUDRED, KADABRA AND QWILFISH.

YOUR FINAL PARTY CONSISTS OF...

EXCUSE ME.

EXCUSE ME...!

I SEE. I SEE.

WHICH WILL HE CHOOSE FIRST?

THORTON MUST PARTICIPATE IN THIS FINAL BATTLE USING RENTAL POKÉMON AS WELL.

OH! PLEASE IGNORE THE NUMBER I JUST SAID.

IT'S NOT A BAD COMBINATION— ABOUT 93%.

BOM

BOM

BATTLE START!

WOOOSSH

THAT'S ONE OF THE MORE POWERFUL DARK-TYPE POKÉMON...

TYRANITAR.

STOMP!

OOSH

THUNK THUNK

94

BATTLE FRONTIER
RULE BOOK

THERE ARE FIVE TYPES OF FACILITIES, EACH WITH A DIFFERENT TYPE OF POKÉMON BATTLE. THE BATTLES ARE FOUGHT ACCORDING TO STRICT RULES. HERE IS SOME MORE DETAILED INFORMATION ABOUT THE RULES AT VARIOUS FACILITIES.

FACILITY RULES
BATTLE FACTORY

AT THE BATTLE FACTORY, THE BATTLES ARE FOUGHT USING RENTAL POKÉMON, NOT YOUR OWN. EVERY TIME A BATTLE ENDS, THE WINNER MAY SWAP THEIR POKÉMON WITH THEIR OPPONENT'S POKÉMON TO CREATE A STRONGER PARTY. THE FRONTIER BRAIN, THORTON, MUST ALSO USE RENTAL POKÉMON WHEN FACING THE CHALLENGER.

TYPE OF BATTLE	NUMBER OF PARTICIPATING POKÉMON	TO RECEIVE THE COMMEMORATIVE PRINT, YOU WILL NEED...
SINGLE	3 POKÉMON (ALL DIFFERENT TYPES)	7×3 SETS =
DOUBLE	4 POKÉMON (ALL DIFFERENT TYPES)	21 CONSECUTIVE WINS

■ HOW TO RENT THE POKÉMON ■

AFTER CHECKING IN TO THE FACILITY, THE CHALLENGER WILL BE PRESENTED WITH SIX POKÉMON TO CHOOSE FROM. THE CHALLENGER MUST CHOOSE THREE OF THESE POKÉMON (FOR BOTH SINGLE AND DOUBLE BATTLES). THE ORDER IN WHICH THE POKÉMON ARE CHOSEN DETERMINES THE ORDER IN WHICH THEY WILL APPEAR IN BATTLE. ADDITIONALLY, BEFORE RENTING YOUR POKÉMON, THE FACILITY STAFF WILL PROVIDE INFORMATION ABOUT YOUR OPPONENT.

Please choose three Pokémon.

▶ Follow the instructions on the automated machines.

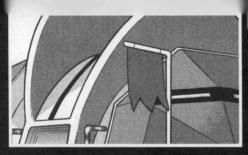

DIRECTIONS

◄ LOCATED AT THE FAR EAST SIDE OF THE BATTLE FRONTIER ENTRANCE, THE FACILITY WITH THE RUGGED LOOKING GATES IS THE BATTLE FACTORY.

■ HOW TO TRADE YOUR POKÉMON ■

AFTER THE BATTLE, YOU MAY SWAP ONE OF YOUR POKÉMON WITH ONE OF YOUR OPPONENT'S POKÉMON. THE WINNER OF THE BATTLE EARNS THE RIGHT TO CHOOSE WHETHER TO TRADE POKÉMON. THIS ENABLES CHALLENGERS TO STRENGTHEN THEIR PARTY AND TESTS THEIR KNOWLEDGE AS TRAINERS. THE POKÉMON YOU CHOOSE WILL MOVE INTO THE POSITION OF THE POKÉMON YOU LET GO.

▲ MAKE SURE TO USE THE MOVES, ABILITIES AND ITEMS OF YOUR OPPONENT'S POKÉMON THAT YOU OBSERVED DURING THE PREVIOUS BATTLE.

◄ THORTON HAS CREATED A TECHNOLOGICAL DEVICE TO EVALUATE HIS OPPONENT'S SKILLS.

BATTLE FRONTIER ❀ | FRONTIER BRAIN **FACTORY HEAD: THORTON**

Adventure 91 ❀ Outlasting Ledian

POKÉMON ADVENTURES

BATTLE CASTLE ...

...FACING THORTON AT THE BATTLE FACTORY AT THIS VERY MOMENT.

I WAS JUST THINKING... I HEARD THAT YOUNG GIRL PLATINUM IS...

THIS ISN'T LIKE YOU.

WHAT'S THE MATTER, DARACH? WHAT ARE YOU STARING AT?

IT'S INCREDIBLE!

SHE ALREADY DEFEATED DAHLIA AS WELL.

I'M SORRY, LADY CAITLIN.

TO TELL YOU THE TRUTH, I...

I'M SORRY.

Woo

IT COMES AS NO SURPRISE THAT YOU'RE INTER- ESTED IN THEIR BATTLE.

IT SURE IS. YOU CAN HEAR THE CHEERING ALL THE WAY OVER HERE.

108

110

BOOM

OH. WELL, YES, I KNOW THAT...

I USED KADABRA AS A RENTAL POKÉMON AND EXPERIENCED IT MYSELF.

WHEN KADABRA USES ITS PSYCHIC POWER, IT EMITS STRONG ALPHA WAVES THAT CAN INTERFERE WITH THE SENSORS OF PRECISION INSTRUMENTS.

GIVE UP AND HAND OVER THE COMMEMORATIVE PRINT, THORTON!

HAR HAR HAR!!

...AND WE'VE JUST FIGURED OUT THAT THE INTERFERENCE IS COMING FROM RADIO WAVES EMITTED FROM SOME SORT OF MACHINE THAT CONTROLS POKÉMON...

OUR COMMUNICATION DEVICES HAVE BEEN DOWN FOR THE PAST SEVERAL HOURS...

HUH?

WHAT DO YOU MEAN?

WE'RE GETTING PRETTY FRUSTRATED TRYING TO TRACK DOWN THE SOURCE OF THIS PROBLEM.

AT LEAST YOUR LITTLE MALFUNCTION ISN'T AS BAD AS OURS.

BATTLE FRONTIER
RULE BOOK

THERE ARE FIVE TYPES OF FACILITIES, EACH WITH A DIFFERENT TYPE OF POKÉMON BATTLE. THE BATTLES ARE FOUGHT ACCORDING TO STRICT RULES. HERE IS SOME MORE DETAILED INFORMATION ABOUT THE RULES AT VARIOUS FACILITIES.

FACILITY RULES
BATTLE HALL

AT THE BATTLE HALL FACILITY, YOU CHOOSE ONE TYPE OF POKÉMON AND WHICH TYPE OF POKÉMON YOU WOULD LIKE TO BATTLE AGAINST. IT WILL BE ONE-ON-ONE FOR A SINGLE BATTLE AND TWO-ON-TWO FOR A DOUBLE BATTLE.

TYPE OF BATTLE	NUMBER OF PARTICIPATING POKÉMON	TO RECEIVE THE COMMEMORATIVE PRINT, YOU WILL NEED...
SINGLE	1 POKÉMON	17 TYPES × 10 RANKS = 170 CONSECUTIVE WINS
DOUBLE	2 POKÉMON (SAME TYPE)	

CHOOSING THE POKÉMON TYPE

THE CHALLENGER FIRST CHOOSES A TYPE OF POKÉMON THEY WANT TO USE IN BATTLE FROM THE 17 POSSIBLE TYPES. EACH BATTLE BEGINS AT RANK I. BY DEFEATING RANK I, YOU MOVE UP TO RANK 2...AND SO ON.

RMAL | RANK FIRE | RANK WATER | RANK ELECT
S | RANK ICE | RANK FIGHTING | RANK POISO
ND | RANK FLYING | RANK PSYCHIC | RANK BUG
| RANK GHOST | RANK DRAGON | RANK DARK

◄ A SINGLE BATTLE WILL BE FOUGHT ONE-ON-ONE. YOU CANNOT SWITCH POKÉMON, SO YOU WILL NOT GET A SECOND CHANCE.

DIRECTIONS

◄ TO GET TO THE FACILITY, WALK DOWN TO THE BATTLE CASTLE IN THE FAR WEST SIDE AND THEN TOWARDS THE BATTLE TOWER TO THE RIGHT.

■ RANK (1-10) ■

THE HIGHEST RANK IS 10. THEREFORE, OPENING THE 10 RANKS FOR THE 17 TYPES EQUALS...17 × 10. THAT'S WHAT THE CHALLENGER MUST AIM FOR. THE TOTAL RECORD OF SUCCESSIVE WINS WILL BE RETAINED AS THE CHALLENGER'S SCORE, AND THE GOAL IS TO SEE HOW MANY CONSECUTIVE WINS THE CHALLENGER CAN EARN WITH THE POKÉMON CHOSEN. THE FRONTIER BRAIN, ARGENTA, WILL APPEAR FOR THE 170TH BATTLE. CHALLENGERS ARE ALLOWED TO USE THEIR OWN ITEMS IN THESE BATTLES.

▲ ALSO, AFTER EVERY TEN WINS, THE CHALLENGER MAY RE-SELECT AN ITEM TO HAND TO THEIR POKÉMON.

BATTLE FRONTIER

FRONTIER BRAIN **HALL MATRON: ARGENTA**

THANK YOU FOR COMING, DARACH.

EXCUSE ME.

I HARDLY EVER SEE YOU ANYMORE... NOT EVEN AT FRONTIER BRAIN MEETINGS.

MY APOLO-GIES.

I'M GRATEFUL YOU MADE TIME TO COME DOWN HERE TODAY.

I DO.

AND I AM LADY CAITLIN'S VALET. PLEASE UNDERSTAND THAT I HAVE MANY DUTIES TO ATTEND TO.

THE BATTLE CASTLE IS AN INDEPENDENT FACILITY OWNED BY LADY CAITLIN.

LADY CAITLIN WAS DEEPLY SHOCKED AFTER READING THE E-MAIL YOU SENT HER. SHE ASKED ME TO PRIORITIZE THIS ABOVE EVERYTHING ELSE.

THE FATE OF THE ENTIRE BATTLE ZONE IS AT STAKE!

BUT OF COURSE.

132

HMM... YOU MUST HAVE THOUGHT USING YOUR FROSLASS WOULD GIVE YOU AN ADVANTAGE OVER A DRAGON-TYPE POKÉMON, BUT...

DON'T THINK YOU'LL BE ABLE TO DEFEAT A RANK 10 POKÉMON JUST BECAUSE YOU HAVE A TYPE ADVANTAGE OVER IT!

...YOU WERE MY ENEMY, REMEMBER?

THE FIRST TIME I MET YOU AT SNOWPOINT GYM...

FROSLASS...

LATER ON, SHE HANDED YOU OVER TO ME AND WE BECAME A TEAM.

SWISH

YOU WERE CANDICE'S POKÉMON AND A FORMIDABLE OPPONENT.

TNK TNK TNK TNK TNK

THE BABIRI BERRY!

HWF

HWF

FLOMP

I SEE... YOU HAD IT ON YOU, DIDN'T YOU? THE BERRY THAT HALVES THE DAMAGE OF SUPER EFFECTIVE MOVES...

HM!?

AH... RIGHT.

MR. PALMER, SHALL WE GET DOWN TO BUSINESS NOW?

SHE'S DEFEATED **ANOTHER** FRONTIER BRAIN!

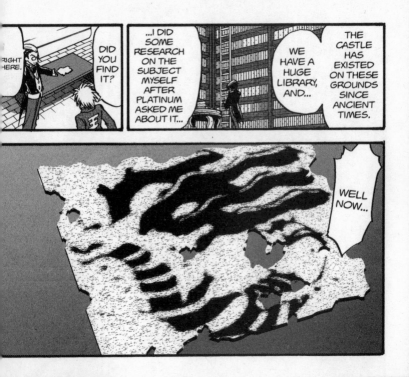

RIGHT
HERE.

DID
YOU
FIND
IT?

...I DID
SOME
RESEARCH
ON THE
SUBJECT
MYSELF
AFTER
PLATINUM
ASKED ME
ABOUT IT...

WE
HAVE A
HUGE
LIBRARY,
AND...

THE
CASTLE
HAS
EXISTED
ON THESE
GROUNDS
SINCE
ANCIENT
TIMES.

WELL
NOW...

DARACH.

...AND ...

THORTON.

AND DARACH SEARCHED THROUGH THE MOUNTAIN OF BOOKS IN THE CASTLE LIBRARY FOR INFORMATION ABOUT THE DISTORTION WORLD.

...TEAM GALACTIC'S SURVEIL-LANCE MACHINE, WHICH RILEY GOT AHOLD OF.

THORTON IS ATTEMPT-ING TO FIX...

HE HELPED PINPOINT THE INTER-FERENCE WITH HIS AURA READING SKILLS.

...THIS IS RILEY FROM IRON ISLAND.

...AND VOLUNTEERED TO HELP.

THEY WERE ALL TOUCHED BY YOUR PASSION...

THE BATTLE FRONTIER IS COMPLETELY ISOLATED FROM THE OUTSIDE WORLD NOW!

IT'S NOT JUST THAT!

IT'S BEEN GETTING WORSE THESE PAST TWO DAYS.

AS YOU KNOW, THE BATTLE FRONTIER HAS BEEN EXPERIENCING SOME TROUBLE WITH ITS COMMUNICATION DEVICES LATELY.

...NOR CAN WE ACCESS THE POKÉMON STORAGE SYSTEM.

WE'RE NOT GETTING ANY RESPONSE WHEN WE HAIL THE SINNOH MAINLAND...

WE CAN'T COMMUNICATE WITH EACH OTHER AT ALL—NOT EVEN FROM ONE FACILITY TO THE NEXT.

YES.

IT'S THAT BAD?!

I MIGHT NOT BE ABLE TO SOLVE THIS ALONE...

I WON'T ALLOW THIS TO HAPPEN ON MY WATCH! IT'S AN OUTRAGE!

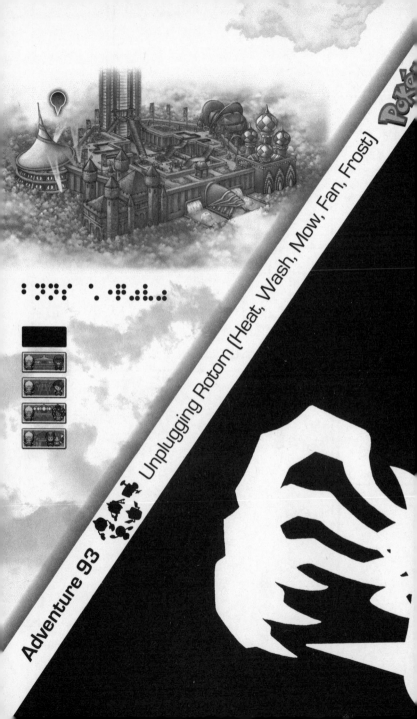

GOT IT!

WELL, TO BEGIN WITH—

We're not a trio! And what's wrong with our clothes?!

THE REAL REASON I FORMED THE ODDLY DRESSED TRIO WITH YOU IS—

ALL RIGHTIE THEN...

ROUTE 205

I ASKED HIM TO. BECAUSE OF THIS...

WHY IS HE COMING WITH US?

GREAT. UH... WE SHOULD GET GOING.

HURRAY! WONDERFUL! ONE BIG FOOTPRINT!

I'VE NAMED HIM REG.

...REGI-GIGAS?!

IS THAT...? COULD IT BE...? A...

LADY SAID IT SNEAKED INTO HER BAG AT SNOWPOINT TEMPLE.

...AFTER THAT...

...IT LOCKED ITSELF INSIDE THIS POKÉ BALL AND IT WON'T COME OUT.

BUT...

IT HELPED US WIN OUR FINAL BATTLE AT THE SPEAR PILLAR.

I WANT HIM TO FIGURE OUT WHAT REG IS FEELING BY STUDYING ITS FOOTPRINT WHEN IT FINALLY COMES OUT OF THE POKÉ BALL.

I SEE.

...DR. FOOT-STEP!

AND THAT'S...

BUT THERE'S ONE PERSON WHO WILL!

I DON'T GET IT.

...MEN-TIONED IN CHARON'S NOTES...

IT'S BECAUSE OF THE LEGENDARY POKÉMON OF THE SINNOH REGION...

RIGHT! ABOUT THAT!

SO WHY ARE YOU REALLY HERE?

I WAS THINKING... IF IT WERE POSSIBLE TO VISIT EACH ONE OF THEM, WE COULD PROTECT THEM OR MOVE THEM OUT OF CHARON'S REACH.

AND ROTOM.

MANA-PHY.

HEAT-RAN.

SHAY-MIN.

CRES-SELIA.

DARK-RAI.

WOW! I'LL GET TO COLLECT SO MANY RARE FOOTPRINTS!

AND I WAS WONDERING IF YOU TWO WOULD HELP ME WITH THAT.

...AS WELL AS THE REPORTS FROM THE ELITE FOUR. THEY ALL MENTION ETERNA FOREST, THE OLD CHATEAU, AND PLASMA. SO I HAVE A HUNCH...

AFTER THE BATTLE AT THE SPEAR PILLAR, I READ THIS PAGE IN CHARON'S NOTE-BOOK...

WE'RE ON THE WAY TO INVESTIGATE ROTOM.

ACTUALLY... PROFES-SOR ROWAN ALREADY ASKED US TO DO HIM A FAVOR.

WHAT? REALLY?

TURNS OUT, WE'VE MET ROTOM BEFORE.

THE OLD CHATEAU ....

THE EDGE OF ETERNA FOREST ...

BUT REALLY IT'S JUST ROTOM...

IT'S SUPPOSED TO BE HAUNTED.

NOW WE CAN FINALLY CHECK OUT ROTOM ONCE AND FOR ALL.

...A MYSTERIOUS PLASMA POKÉMON WHO MOVES FROM ONE ELECTRICAL APPLIANCE TO ANOTHER.

THIS PLACE STILL GIVES ME THE CREEPS, PEARL.

YEAH... TO BE HONEST, I'M FEELING PRETTY JITTERY MYSELF.

OKAY. ...AND YOU EVEN MANAGED TO CALM IT DOWN. I WOULD LIKE YOU TO SHOW ME MORE OF YOUR CLEVER IDEAS!

...AND YOU FIGURED OUT THAT IT WOULD RETURN TO THAT TV...

SO ROTOM LIVES INSIDE THE TELEVISION...

HEY, YOU'RE THE ONE WHO BLABBED TO PROFESSOR ROWAN!

BUT IF ROTOM REMEMBERS US...WE WON'T BE ABLE TO USE THE SAME TRICK AS LAST TIME.

AT SANDGEM TOWN AFTER THE FINAL BATTLE AT THE SPEAR PILLAR...

WHAT?

DID I SAY THAT?

YOU DID!

AND ONLY BETWEEN 8:00 IN THE EVENING AND SUN-UP.

WE DON'T HAVE A CHOICE! ROTOM ONLY APPEARS AT NIGHT!

WHY DIDN'T WE COME DURING THE DAY?

AHH!

AHH!!

CREEEEEPY

AT ANY RATE...

SQUEEEK

LET'S OPEN THE DOOR...

READY...

THE TV IN THIS ROOM WAS ITS LAIR, RIGHT?

RSP R S P

ROTOM CAN ENTER MACHINES...

... BECAUSE ITS BODY IS COMPOSED OF PLASMA.

YES! IT'S JUST LIKE THE POKÉDEX SAYS!

R SP

FOUND IT!!

FOUND IT! FOUND IT!

COME OUT, COME OUT, WHEREVER YOU ARE!

Rotom
Species: Plasma Pokémon
Type: Electric/Ghost

Height: Height: 1' 00"
Weight: Weight: 0.7 lbs

OKAY...

Its electric-like body can enter some kinds of machines and take control in order to make mischief.

WHAT'S THIS?

HM...

AT ANY RATE, LET'S HEAD DOWN THERE!

HMM...

MAYBE IT HAS SOMETHING TO DO WITH THE BUILDING ROTOM WENT INTO?

IT'S GOT ETERNA CITY WRITTEN ON IT TOO.

...RIGHT? I GUESS THAT MEANS IT'S A SECRET KEY...

SECRET KEY

SPEAKING OF POKÉMON!

SPEAKING OF POKÉMON!

159

AND THEY ALL HAVE A STRANGELY SHAPED MOTOR ATTACHED TO THEM.

I WONDER WHAT THESE ARE?

A REFRIGERATOR, ELECTRIC FAN...

WHAT IS THIS PLACE?

A LAWN MOWER AND WASHING MACHINE.

AND A MICROWAVE TOO. IT'S LIKE...AN *ELECTRIC APPLIANCE STORE.*

OVERHEAT!

FOOM

...AFTER IT ENTERS A MACHINE, IT'S ABLE TO USE A MOVE THAT CHARACTERIZES THAT MACHINE.

BOINK

ROTOM'S BODY IS MADE OF PLASMA, SO IT CAN ENTER ALL KINDS OF ELECTRICAL APPLIANCES. THEN...

I'VE GOT IT, DIA! I'VE FIGURED OUT WHY ROTOM IS A SPECIAL POKÉMON!

VWOOP

IT'S POINTLESS TO STRATEGIZE ABOUT WHAT TYPE OF POKÉMON WE SHOULD USE AGAINST IT—SINCE ITS TYPE IS ALWAYS CHANGING!

169

I DON'T THINK ROTOM WAS CHALLENGING US TO A POKÉMON BATTLE AFTER ALL.

OH, HI, PEARL.

DON'T YOU "HUH" ME! HOW COME YOU'RE NAPPING WITH ROTOM?! WHERE DID YOUR SHIRT AND PANTS GO?

HUH?

HEY! WAKE UP, DIA!

IT SEEMED LIKE IT WANTED TO SHOW ME SOMETHING, SO I LOOKED CLOSELY AND NOTICED IT HAD MOWED THE LAWN IN THE SHAPE OF MY FACE.

MOW ROTOM STOPPED ALL OF A SUDDEN... AFTER RUNNING AROUND FOR A WHILE WITH ME ON ITS BACK.

IT GRILLED BERRIES FOR ME, MADE ME ICE CREAM, AND EVEN WASHED AND DRIED MY CLOTHES!

SO I ASKED ROTOM TO DO ALL KINDS OF STUFF FOR ME... AND IT WAS TOTALLY INTO IT.

...MAYBE ROTOM BROUGHT US HERE TO SHOW OFF ITS POWERS.

AND THAT'S WHEN I STARTED THINKING...

DUNNO. I CAN'T TELL HOW MANY DAYS HAVE PASSED... WHETHER IT'S DAY OR NIGHT... WHICH WAY IS UP OR DOWN...

I WON-DER HOW LONG IT'S BEEN.

YEAH.

YOU HEAR ME, BRO?

BATTLE FRONTIER
RULE BOOK

THERE ARE FIVE TYPES OF
FACILITIES, EACH WITH A DIFFERENT
TYPE OF POKÉMON BATTLE. THE
BATTLES ARE FOUGHT ACCORDING
TO STRICT RULES. HERE IS SOME
MORE DETAILED INFORMATION
ABOUT THE RULES AT VARIOUS
FACILITIES.

FACILITY RULES
BATTLE TOWER

THE BATTLE TOWER IS A FACILITY WHERE YOU CAN ENJOY A STANDARD
POKÉMON BATTLE FIGHTING SEVEN OPPONENTS IN A ROW. THE GOAL
IS TO BUILD UP AS MANY CONSECUTIVE WINS AS YOU CAN.

TYPE OF BATTLE	NUMBER OF PARTICIPATING POKÉMON	TO RECEIVE THE COMMEMORATIVE PRINT, YOU WILL NEED...
SINGLE	3 POKÉMON (ALL DIFFERENT TYPES)	7×7 SETS =
DOUBLE	4 POKÉMON (ALL DIFFERENT TYPES)	49 CONSECUTIVE WINS

■ITEMS■

YOU ARE ALLOWED TO BRING YOUR OWN
ITEMS WITH YOU TO THIS FACILITY. ALL
THREE POKÉMON FIGHTING IN A SINGLE
BATTLE, AND ALL FOUR POKÉMON
FIGHTING IN A DOUBLE BATTLE MAY BE
EQUIPPED WITH AN ITEM (RESTRICTION:
ALL THE POKÉMON MUST BE EQUIPPED
WITH A DIFFERENT ITEM.)

◀▲THIS BUILDING WAS DESIGNED
TO TEST POKÉMON BATTLE SKILLS.

DIRECTIONS

◄ THE SYMBOL OF THE BATTLE FRONTIER IS LOCATED AT THE BACK AND CAN BE SEEN FROM EVERYWHERE.

■ ACHIEVEMENT TROPHIES AND RIBBONS ■

UNLIKE THE OTHER FOUR FACILITIES, THE BATTLE TOWER AWARDS TROPHIES AND RIBBONS TO HIGH-ACHIEVING TRAINERS. THE TROPHIES ARE THE GOLD TROPHY, SILVER TROPHY AND BRONZE TROPHY. THE RIBBONS ARE THE ABILITY RIBBON, GREAT ABILITY RIBBON AND SO FORTH. CHALLENGE YOURSELF TO TRY AND ACQUIRE THESE ALONG WITH THE COMMEMORATIVE PRINT.

▲ THIS SYSTEM IDENTIFIES THE BEST OF THE BEST TRAINERS.

BATTLE FRONTIER

FRONTIER BRAIN **TOWER TYCOON: PALMER**

WHAT IS THE DISTORTION WORLD?!

A PICTURE OF THIS MYSTERIOUS WORLD IS GRADUALLY STARTING TO EMERGE BY PIECING TOGETHER CHARON'S WORDS, HIS WRITINGS IN HIS NOTEBOOK, AND THE INFORMATION PLATINUM HAS GATHERED AT THE BATTLE ZONE. AN EERIE WORLD LIES ON THE OTHER SIDE OF THAT HOLE!

GIRATINA HAS FINALLY APPEARED! AND NOW THE CONFLICT MOVES TO THE MAIN STAGE— THE DISTORTION WORLD! WE ATTEMPT A THOROUGH ANALYSIS OF THAT MYSTERIOUS REALM IN THE FOLLOWING PAGES...

AKA THE "OTHER SIDE OF THE WORLD"

THE DISTORTION WORLD EXISTS IN A REALM THAT IS USUALLY NOT VISIBLE TO US. DAHLIA AND CHARON DESCRIBED IT AS THE "OTHER SIDE OF THE WORLD."

▲ A GLIMPSE OF THE "OTHER SIDE" CAN BE SEEN THROUGH THIS HOLE. TENTACLES STRETCH OUT AND GRAB ANYTHING THEY TOUCH.

CONNECTIONS TO TEAM GALACTIC'S MACHINE.

VEILSTONE CITY: DIA AND PEARL SAW THIS PIECE OF TECHNOLOGY DURING THEIR FIRST BATTLE AGAINST TEAM GALACTIC. THE MYSTERIOUS ENERGY USED BY THIS MACHINE APPEARS TO HAVE SOMETHING IN COMMON WITH THE DISTORTION WORLD.

▲ THE MACHINE APPEARED OUT OF THE ROOF OF THE BUILDING! ON SATURN'S ORDERS, "ABSOLUTE TERROR" WAS UNLEASHED!

THE CONCEPT OF TIME AND SPACE

HOW DOES TIME PASS IN THE DISTORTION WORLD? HOW LARGE IS IT? IT'S SAID THAT THE LAWS OF PHYSICS DON'T APPLY IN THIS WORLD, THAT TIME AND SPACE ARE DISTORTED... IT'S LIKELY THAT THE DISTORTION WORLD WAS NAMED FOR THESE ANOMALIES.

▼ A PARTIAL DISTORTION. COULD THERE BE A WORLD WHERE THE DISTORTION IS EVEN WORSE...?

▼ THE WORD "ANTIMATTER" IS WRITTEN IN CHARON'S NOTES. WHAT DOES IT REFER TO?

THE TWO DRAGON-TYPE POKÉMON AND CYRUS WERE DRAGGED INTO THE DISTORTION WORLD BY GIRATINA. PAKA AND UJI WERE WRENCHED INTO THE DISTORTION WORLD BY TEAM GALACTIC'S MYSTERIOUS MACHINE. WILL THEY EVER BE REUNITED WITH OUR FRIENDS...?"

WHERE ARE THE PEOPLE AND POKÉMON WHO GOT DRAGGED INTO THE DISTORTION WORLD...?!

Height	22' 08"
Weight	1433.0 lbs.
Species	Renegade Pokémon
Gender	Unknown
Type	Ghost-Dragon
Ability	Levitate
Pokédex Number	Sinnoh: 210, National: 487
Held Item	Griseous Orb

THE ONLY LIFE-FORM THAT LIVES INSIDE THE DISTORTION WORLD IS THE POKÉMON GIRATINA! GIRATINA ONCE LIVED IN OUR WORLD. ACCORDING TO ANCIENT RECORDS, IT MOVED TO THE DISTORTION WORLD AFTER BEING EXILED FROM OURS FOR BEHAVING LIKE A TYRANT. WHAT IS IT THINKING ABOUT? AND WHAT ARE ITS SHARP EYES EXAMINING SO INTENSELY?

GIRATINA

GIRATINA

DIALGA

PALKIA

CYRUS

PAKA & UJI

AND ITS INCREDIBLE NEW LOOK!!

Message from
Hidenori Kusaka

Everybody has their weaknesses. My obvious one is distinguishing between right and left. I don't have any problems when I take a moment to think about it, but it's hard for me to figure out which is which when I suddenly hear "right" or "left." Even when I'm riding in a taxi, I'll tell the driver, "Please take a left" when I actually want to go right. And when I want to go left, I tell the driver, "Please take a right." I end up saying the opposite of what I mean. This problem has given me a lot of trouble during my road training for my driver's license. So in order to overcome this weakness... (To be continued in vol. 11...)

Message from
Satoshi Yamamoto

I usually draw my characters in extremes. That's because I enjoy exaggerated characters... I want even the minor characters to leave a lasting impression in the minds of readers. I assume that readers understand my love of these minor characters when they vote for them in popularity polls...even though I only exaggerate them for kicks. (LOL)

More Adventures Coming Soon...

The battle rages back and forth between the Distortion World and the regul
world! Then, when Legendary Pokémon Giratina attacks Pearl, Dia interven
with disastrous consequences! Meanwhile, Lady finds an unexpected ally in
an unexpected location.

Will peace ever be restored to the Sinnoh region...?!

Plus, spend time with lots of Pokémon including Blissey, Giratina, Regigigas
Slowking, Rotom, Shaymin, Cresselia, Magmortar, Electivire, Alakazam,
Tangrowth and Arcanine!

CATCH THE EXCITING CONCLUSION!

AVAILABLE NOW!

POKÉMON™

ADVENTURES
HEARTGOLD & SOULSILVER

by HIDENORI KUSAKA
SATOSHI YAMAMOTO

In this **two-volume** thriller, troublemaker Gold and feisty Silver must team up again to find their old enemy Lance and the Legendary Pokémon Arceus!

Available now!

POKÉMON
™

●SUN & MOON

Story
Hidenori Kusaka

Art
Satoshi Yama

Sun dreams of money. Moon dreams o
scientific discoveries. When their paths c
with Team Skull, both their plans go awr

**PICK UP YOUR COPY AT YOUR
LOCAL BOOK STORE.**

POKéMON

Ω RUBY · α SAPPHIRE
OMEGA   ALPHA

BY
...ENORI KUSAKA

Y
...OSHI YAMAMOTO

...ome adventures inspired by the best-selling
...mon Omega Ruby and Pokémon Alpha Sapphire
... games that pick up where the *Pokémon Adventures*
& Sapphire saga left off!

viz media
viz.com

RATED
A
FOR
ALL AGES

Pokémon

HORIZON
SUN & MOON

Akira's summer vacation in the Alola region heats up when he befriends a Rockruff with a mysterious gemstone. Together, Akira hopes they can achieve his newfound dream of becoming a Pokémon Trainer and master the amazing Z-Move. But first, Akira needs to pass a test to earn a Trainer Passport. This becomes more difficult when Rockruff gets kidnapped! And then Team Kings shows up with—you guessed it—evil plans for world domination!

Story & Art
TENYA YAB

THIS IS THE END OF THIS GRAPHIC NOVEL!

To properly enjoy this VIZ Media graphic novel, please turn it around and begin reading from right to left.

This book has been printed in the original Japanese format in order to preserve the orientation of the original artwork. Have fun with it!

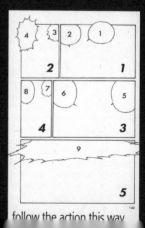

follow the action this way